cl♣verleaf books™

Community Helpers

Let's Meet a Dentist

Bridget Heos

illustrated by Kyle Poling

M MILLBROOK PRESS · MINNEAPOLIS

With thanks to Dr. Erin Flood —B.H.

Text and illustrations copyright © 2013 by Lerner Publishing
Group, Inc.

Millbrook Press
A division of Lerner Publishing Group, Inc.
241 First Avenue North
Minneapolis, MN 55401 U.S.A.

Website address: www.lernerbooks.com

Main body text set in Slappy Inline 18/28.
Typeface provided by T26.

Library of Congress Cataloging-in-Publication Data

Heos, Bridget.
    Let's meet a dentist / by Bridget Heos ; illustrated by Kyle
Poling.
        p.   cm. — (Cloverleaf books™ — community helpers)
    Includes index.
    ISBN 978-0-7613-9029-9 (lib. bdg. : alk. paper)
    1. Dentists—Juvenile literature. 2. Dentistry—Juvenile
literature. I. Poling, Kyle, ill. II. Title.
RK63.H46 2013
617.6—dc23   2012023074

Manufactured in the United States of America
1 – BP – 12/31/12

TABLE OF CONTENTS

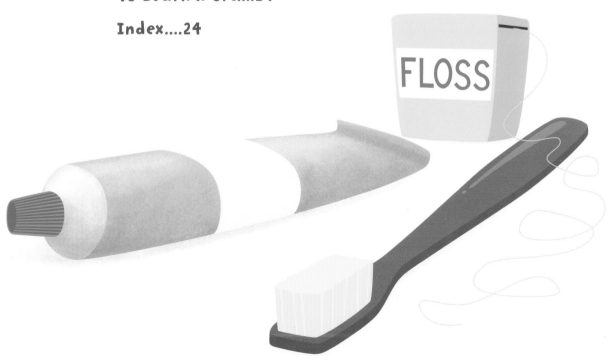

Chapter One

Four Hundred Teeth

Our class is on a mission! We want to find out what a **dentist** does. We visit a dentist named Dr. Florez at her office.

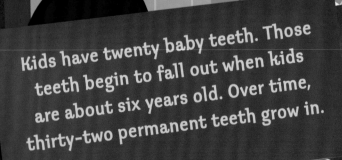

Kids have twenty baby teeth. Those teeth begin to fall out when kids are about six years old. Over time, thirty-two permanent teeth grow in.

"I help people **care for their teeth**," Dr. Florez says. She tells us she sees about twenty patients every day. That's more than four hundred teeth! No wonder it feels crowded in here.

SIGN IN

We ask how she cares for all those teeth. Dr. Florez takes us to an **exam room**. First, she puts on gloves and a mask. Those help **stop germs** from spreading.

Dr. Florez lets Jasmine sit in the chair. It moves up and down. "Do you play in the chair?" asks Jacob.

"No," says Dr. Florez. "But I'm glad you think it's fun."

Dentists are workers in the community. A community is a group of people who live in the same city, town, or neighborhood.

Dr. Florez says her helper, Pam, cleans each patient's teeth. Pam **scrapes gunk off** with special tools.

A hygienist is trained to clean teeth and help the dentist.

Dr. Florez shows us a small machine she calls a "slow speed." She steps on a pedal. The slow speed spins. Pam puts toothpaste on the tip. She uses it to **polish** the patient's teeth. "Once the teeth are clean, I take a look," says Dr. Florez.

Chapter Two

Attack of the Sugar Bugs!

Dr. Florez holds up a **tiny mirror** and something she calls an **explorer**. "These help me find cavities. Cavities are holes in your teeth," she says. She moves the explorer along the teeth. If it gets stuck in a tooth, there is a hole.

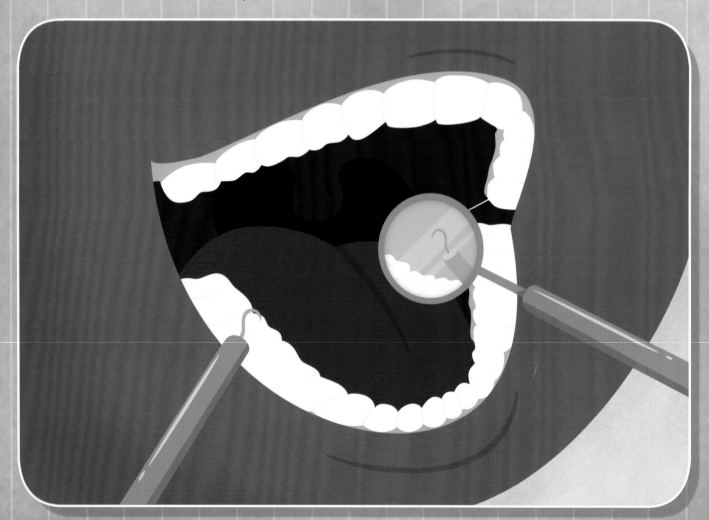

She points to **X-rays of teeth**. They show cavities between the teeth, she explains. "They also show me the parts of your teeth hidden below the gums."

"Do cavities really come from bacteria pooping?" asks Robert. Most of us laugh. So does Dr. Florez.

"That's right," says Dr. Florez. "Germs called **bacteria** eat food left on your teeth. They leave acid behind as waste, like poop. The acid makes holes in your teeth."

"**Gross!**" we say.

"That's why I tell people to brush and floss every day. **Clean teeth don't have food for bacteria.**"
She shows us a poster about keeping teeth healthy.

HOW TO KEEP YOUR TEETH HAPPY

*Brush your teeth once after breakfast and once before bed.

*Brush for two whole minutes.

*Floss every night before bed.

*Avoid sweet drinks and foods.

*See the dentist twice a year.

Bacteria love to eat sugar left on your teeth. So sugary snacks and drinks can lead to more cavities.

"When a tooth has a hole in it, I put in a **filling**," says Dr. Florez. She shows us white and silver fillings. "The filling starts out soft. I push it into the cavity. It hardens when it dries."

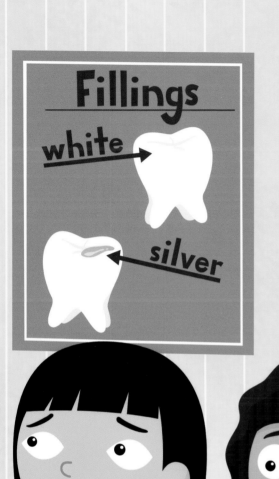

Fillings

white →

silver →

"Ouch," says Olivia.

"We give you medicine so it doesn't hurt," says Dr. Florez. "In fact, it feels better. Bad cavities cause toothaches."

If you don't have a dentist, ask your school counselor or nurse about free dental clinics in your area. Dentists will clean your teeth and check for cavities.

She uses a chart to keep track of each patient's teeth. She writes how many **permanent teeth** young patients have. She also notes any **cavities.**

Molars are the twelve teeth grown-ups have that young kids don't. They are in the back of the mouth. The farthest back molars are called wisdom teeth. They are often removed. So many adults have twenty-eight teeth instead of thirty-two.

Chapter Three

Straighten Up, Teeth

"What else do you do?" asks Ryan.

"I check to see if kids need braces," she says. "Sometimes teeth grow in **crooked** or don't line up well. Then you see an orthodontist. That dentist straightens teeth with braces or retainers."

Some of us can't wait to get **braces.**

Most dental hygienists go to college for two years. Dentists go to college for four years. Then they go to dental school for four more. Orthodontists go to school an extra two years.

It's time to go back to school.

"Take good care of your teeth, and they will stick around," says Dr. Florez. "I have a patient who is one hundred years old. He still has twenty-eight healthy teeth!"

Because Dr. Florez lends a hand to make our teeth healthy, we give *her* a hand.

Make an Apple Mouth Snack

Sugary snacks can cause cavities. Fun snacks can still be healthy, like this one. Brushing and flossing your teeth before bedtime will make sure popcorn bits and juice from the apples don't stick to your teeth overnight.

Ingredients:
2 slices of apple with red or pink skin
1 tablespoon peanut butter (or honey in case of nut allergies)
½ cup plain popped popcorn

1. Spread peanut butter (or honey) on one white side of both apple slices.

2. Break up the popcorn into twenty smaller pieces.

3. Push ten pieces of popcorn into the peanut butter or honey on each slice.

4. Put the two slices together with the popcorn forming two rows of teeth. The apple skins are like lips!

Enjoy the apple slices as a snack. Don't forget to brush and floss your own teeth later!

GLOSSARY

acid: a sour-tasting substance that can break down other substances

baby teeth: the first set of teeth a child has. These start to grow when a person is about six months old.

bacteria: one-celled living things that live in or on other living things. Some bacteria live in people's mouths and make acid from food left on teeth.

cavity: a hole in a tooth

dentist: a person who cares for teeth and diagnoses and treats problems with the teeth and gums

explorer: a pointed tool that a dentist uses to feel for cavities

floss: string used to clean between teeth

hygienist: a trained worker who cleans teeth and takes X-rays of teeth

molars: the twelve teeth at the back of the mouth that are designed to chew food

mouth mirror: a metal tool with a mirror on the end, used to see inside the mouth

orthodontist: a dentist specializing in moving teeth, usually with retainers or braces

permanent teeth: the set of teeth that grows in beginning when a person is about six years old

root: the part of the tooth attached to the gums

slow speed: a handheld machine that spins and is used to polish teeth

X-ray: an image taken of an area inside the body, such as teeth

BOOKS

Cobb, Vicki. *Your Body Battles a Cavity.* Minneapolis: Millbrook Press, 2009.
Want to see what cavity-causing bacteria look like when magnified twenty-two thousand times? Illustrations and magnified photos in this book show how your mouth fights back (with help from your dentist).

Heos, Bridget. *Let's Meet a Doctor.* Minneapolis: Millbrook Press, 2013.
Learn about being a pediatrician—a doctor for kids. Dr. Zambil visits a classroom to talk about how he helps people and the tools he uses.

Humphrey, Paul. *My Visit to the Dentist.* New York: Franklin Watts, 2008.
Read more about what to expect when you visit a dentist.

WEBSITES

Give Kids a Smile
http://www.ada.org/givekidsasmile
Find out about free dental care for kids who need it.

Kids' Health—Your Teeth
http://kidshealth.org/kid/htbw/teeth.html
Learn about taking care of your teeth and
the strange ways people used to care for their teeth.

To Tell the Tooth
http://www.ada.org/380.aspx
Test your knowledge on taking care of your teeth with this trivia game!

LERNER SOURCE™

Expand learning beyond the printed book. Download free, complementary educational resources for this book from our website, www.lerneresource.com.